Brief Garden

By the same author:

Poetry
small rebellions (1984)
Flight of Koalas (1993)
The Pomelo Tree (2001)
Coast (2005)
How Like the Past (2009)
Barnacle Rock (2014)
Sri Lanka Journey (2017)

Anthologies
(co-ed.) *Midday Horizon: First Choice of Australian Poets* (1996)
(ed.) *Antipodes: poetic responses* (2011)
(ed.) *Caring for Country: poetic responses* (2017)

Brief Garden

Margaret Bradstock

PUNCHER & WATTMANN

First published in 2019
Published by Puncher and Wattmann
PO Box 279
Waratah NSW 2298

http://www.puncherandwattmann.com
puncherandwattmann@bigpond.com

NATIONAL
LIBRARY
OF AUSTRALIA

ISBN   9781925780413

Cover design by Miranda Douglas

Printed by Lightning Source International

This project has been assisted by the
Australian Government through the
Australia Council, its arts funding and
advisory body.

Australian Government

Australia Council
for the Arts

Contents

I

II

III

I

The Navigators

There are many seas, organ-pipe rocks.
Sometimes we drift for months, and wake
    to the dog-watch of the night,
on our lips the bitterest taste of land.

Our anchor-snared ship
      perched on the ocean's skin,
we hear the hull's creak, keening
of the lines, fancy we hear voices
         through the thunder of waves
knowing they're the cries of sea-birds,
the boom and boom of breakers upon rock.

Cloudlands rise from the mist
saw-toothed peaks emptied into the sky
      vanishing as we approach
the sun's glare, a shifting sea
with nothing at its centre, the motion
        of a rocking island.

William Hodges – *View in Pickersgill Harbour, Dusky Bay* ca.1776

Failing three times to enter through the Heads
Cook sailed *Resolution* into Dusky Sound
                     anchoring in Pickersgill Harbour
the crew at rest after their Antarctic voyage
            the ship in need of repairs
     an acre of forest cleared on Astronomer's Point
to push back the wilderness.

Hodges' painting of Dusky Bay, backlit
with new-world promise, is stripped
               of rainforest clutter, trees spread out
like English Oaks in pastoral graciousness.
Felled branches stretch from ship to shore
        a makeshift gangplank still in leaf
two seamen making landfall.

Rainforest gives way to a different canvas
             as x-rays of the artwork reveal icebergs
erupting like grey and white volcanoes
                into a rowdy sea, then painted over
(a palimpsest in whited-out palette)
       the first known sketches of Antarctica's terrain.
Perspective shows *Resolution*'s sloping deck
a ghost-ship in the background, inserted
             dumbstruck, into that ice-bound frame.

Watkin Tench at the river (1791)

It was always about the fish.
Our British sailors fished their waters,
              their livelihood, as if they were
our own. By night the natives
             thieve from our potato patch
and spear our sheep.   How do you
put a name to 'ownership' or 'rights'?

We barter with words
shining like mirrors or glass beads
              but meaningless without
the geometry of language,
                its intricate flight
a gilded bird, caught by the sun's
            first rays, across the blue of sky.

We live nearly three years at Port Jackson
      before learning that *beèal* signifies 'no'
and not 'good'.

Our natives and the stranger tribes
             speak different dialects
but understand each other perfectly,
the same customs, common ground.
        Asked 'Where's Rose Hill? Where?'
they throw up their hands and utter
          a sound denoting distance.

A shallow wooded valley runs back
into the country. Here the water shifts,
        two ducks crossing from one point
to another, a circular ripple

multiplies out and out,
ring after perfect ring. Somewhere
on the far bank, a bird makes the same sound
over and over.

Past Richmond Hill, a cleft in the rock
known to those who've been up the Hawkesbury
tells us we've gone too far, sends us
back to this view of nothing
but trees growing on precipices, *to this pile*
of desolation...His Excellency was pleased
to name Tench's Prospect Mount.

The last bush falls away and I stand
on top of the dune, looking out on the bay
and the land, at this tributary
we name the Nepean. Standing there
on the earth, at the same time watching
from somewhere beyond, is
like trying to think in two languages,
looking for patterns.

The Sealers, Preservation Island

– George Augustus Robinson, 1830

By what irony was this island
            named a safe harbour
after the wreck of the *Sydney Cove*?
Here the sealers hold sway
            ex-convicts and scum of the system
wives kidnapped from native tribes
tied to the trees and flogged
    their copper-skinned offspring slave labour.
Rather than hand them this life
women murder the children
            stuffing their mouths with sand.

Rivers of moonbirds hang over the rescue-boat
flow to the sea, the rocky foreshores,
            past islands of tussock grass
teeming rookeries of seals and sea lions
there for the taking, a miasma
of clubbing and skinning
        the scrimshaw of discarded bone.

With the sealers out on the straits
the women are up at the bird rookery
      gathering firewood, strolling downhill
reluctant to leave the dogs. Once on our boat
the *Charlotte*, they laugh and sing
        glad to be free of their masters.

The smell of bloodshed clings about these islands.

The Black Line

' …*to effect the voluntary removal of the entire black population…to place every last one of them on Flinders Island*' – George Augustus Robinson (Conciliator of Aborigines, 1832)

1.

Walking once more by the river
                          conjuring the moment
things might have been different, I wonder

why I am known as *a Victorian do-gooder*
yet achieved so little good.
Even as Arthur's Black Line surged downwards

martial law declared, the bush
flickering with guard fires, his dragnet capturing
only one man and a boy, it had begun.

Better Truganini had not ferried me to safety
                  across the Welcome River on a log
when the Port Davey mob attacked with spears.

2.

We journeyed south-east from our base camp
opposite Swan Island, crossed Tomahawk River
                  and the Montagu, pursuing a course
to the end of the Western Bluff.

With me chief Manna-largenna, recruited
from Hobart Town gaol, Truganini and Wooraddy
nine other aboriginals and two white men
                earth's shadow on the face of the moon
our foreboding. Truganini insists it's Manna-largenna
killed by the Stoney Creek tribe
                and gone up to the moon.

Smoke spiralling from treetops
sighted by our natives, we come to the campfire
of Umarrah, and the last of his melancholy tribe
        their women stolen by sealers.
They signal for peace and join us.

I sleep in the open, within a ring
                of acrid natives, heartily tired
of this sort of life, my stomach gaseous
unsettled from the stringy wild game.

3.

Frenchman's Cap   its grim volcanic cone
rising thousands of feet above the plain
almost a living thing, with moods of its own
colours of the ice changing
                with every shift of the light.

For seven successive days we travel on
through snowy plateaus and passes
                often waist-deep in the snow
a miserable journey, for our last roundup
        a man, four women and a boy.

The Hobart Town *Courier* gives due thanks
(*the removal of these blacks will be of essential
benefit to themselves and the colony*)
        farewells them all to Flinders Island
religious instruction, shell-fishing and kangaroo hunts
to occupy their minds.

Yet the settlement becomes a prison camp.
They die of floggings, ill health, homesickness
        more shadow than savage crow.

The Whispering Bones

William Lanney, survivor of Wybelenna camp, d.1869 of cholera.

King Billy's dead, Kater has his head,
Sevitt has his hands and feet.
My feet, my feet, my poor black feet
That used to be so gritty,
They're not aboard the Runnymede
They're somewhere in this city .
– popular song, Hobart Town

Dr Crowther took away my head
lowering it from the dead-house window
slipping a white man's under the black skin
        to mask the theft, my bloated features
further distorted *with a lipless grin.*

Measured precisely, wrapped in a sealskin bundle
shipped off to London Town, my skull
my precious skull, was jettisoned
                when it began to stink
wandering the world like an unburied ghost.

Thoughts of possession cluster round dead limbs.
Officials then chopped off my feet and hands
for safe-keeping, trundling them down
            to Salamanca Place or, rumour has it,
the Anglo-Australian Guano Company.

Coffin shrouded in the Union Jack
(sealed with dispensary wax and found brass stamp)
shouldered by whalers from *Runnymede* and *Aladdin*,
            my lopped and bloodied trunk
together with a stranger's flayed head

was buried
exhumed by body-snatchers the next day.
Kater's tobacco pouch (a wondrous thing)
      crafted from my skin, the rest dissected
for its skeleton, which disappeared.

What am I now, seeded into the land
like winter crops, my disembodied voices
calling the limbs and skeleton back home,
      the ache of a cranium
my people's avatar.

Henry Whalley, Chief Harpooner (1819-1877)

His mother was Aboriginal, abducted
to Kangaroo Island by sealers or whalers,
        his father unofficial 'Governor' there.
When the South Australia Company
 took over their Cygnet River farm
        young Henry (like his father before him)
was destined for life at sea.

The whalers were known as hard men
but he was *a favourite with all on board*
... *of great courage and self-reliance.*
        The fetor of rotting meat hanging
over the islands, the reeking and storm-
battered ships, were all part of the job,
        the contest between man and whale,
and the ocean, his reason for being there.

A seabird's eye for the whale pods
arriving from Antarctica each frozen winter
unerring aim, and the shared struggle
                to winch the whale in,
helped nail his reputation. He boarded the ship
Bencleugh on its way to Macquarie Island,
the coastline of violent waters
                known to sailors as Hell's Gates.

Winds roaring in from the Southern Ocean
with a savage storm, shipwrecked the *Bencleugh*
on the shores of the island. Horizontal icicles
        clung to the wreck in the bitter cold,
and he'd broken his hip. Whalley's shipmates
hauled him ashore, hand-over-hand

through the breakers, then carried him northward
        to some weather-worn sealers' huts.

He died, a strange sleep he never woke up from.
When they dug down to bury him, they struck
        the ribs of an old-fashioned sailing vessel
deep under the shingle, an unknown 'waif of the sea'
        from another era, two centuries before
navigating blind, in search of a continent.

Scott's Dream

A confused sea, shifting ice-sheets
glazed frost on the ship, on every fibre of rope.
A huge iceberg sails past, one end
            of the Cape Barne Glacier, perhaps.
I would like to witness the birth of a glacier.

Ponting with his camera recording,
next moment the floe heaves up beneath him,
splits into fragments. I hear the booming noise
            as whale after whale rises under the ice
striking with their backs, setting it rocking.
Such deliberate cunning, the feral, terrible teeth
                        skirting the edges of floes.

                    *

Here in the ice-cave
a crevasse in a tilted berg,
the strata on either side bend outwards.
Through a screen of blue icicles
like prison bars, my body itself a cage,
                past and future haze together
a view of the ship, the western mountains,
a purple sky, and always the Pole.
I dream of killer whales, a recurrent nightmare.
Out on the decaying ice, we're attacked by skuas
                beating at us with their wings.

                    *

A march south of Shackleton's final camp,
less than 40 miles from the Pole now,
the drift snow like finest flour.
Bowers makes out a black speck ahead
flag tied to a sledge bearer, the remains
of the Norwegian camp, sledge tracks crossing
ski tracks, trace of dogs' paws — many dogs.
The Pole. Yes, but under very different circumstances
from those expected.
We build a cairn, raise *our poor slighted Union Jack*
and photograph ourselves.

                    *

Eternal silence of the great white desert
mottled wet green walls of our tent
ceaseless rattle of fluttering canvas.
Evans dead, Oates walking out into
            a sea of storm-tossed sastrugi
and the blizzard thick as a hedge.
We have 30 opium tabloids apiece...
enough, if needed.

It seems a pity, but I do not think
I can write more.

Barangaroo and the Eora fisherwomen

Ahh … we were fisherwomen
food providers for the tribe
fishing from bark canoes (nowie)
with lines and hooks. Twisting together
two strands from kurrajong trees,
cabbage trees or flax, we made our lines,
fish hooks (burra) honed from the turban shell
our working tools, our power.

Skimming the waters in those bark canoes,
fires lit on clay pads for warmth and cooking,
dominating the coastline, they surged
through surf that terrified the sailors. They sang,
kept time with the paddles as they rowed
all day, all weathers, at night.

Eora children grew up on the water,
knowing the sea's voice from their babyhood,
the swell of waves, rocking of the tides
familiar as a mother's heartbeat.
Girls learned to line-fish −
knew the fishing places and songs,
how to hone their crescent *burra*,
when to burley with chewed cockle.

Barangaroo was feisty, wearing a bone
through her nose like a warrior, rebelling
when white sailors sent a load of netted salmon
to her tribesmen as a gift.
She gave birth alone in the forest
spurning the government hospital.

Her baby daughter, Dilboong
did not long survive her, did not receive
                the basket of her fishing gear
laid on the funeral pyre. Tribeswomen
fished the harbour waters for another thirty years
                shooting the waves in their skiffs,
small plumes of smoke rising
                                from onboard fires.

Walking on the headland reserve
                set aside as green space, water views,
glimpses of a forgotten past, before
the lengthening shadow of Crown Casino
                                encroaches on our foreshores
you might imagine them, scudding across the bay
                                still singing.

*Ahh ... what has been done to us
                our paradise of waters.*

II

Progenitor

(William Bragge, 1797-1861)

Arrested on his wedding day,
receiving and carrying away the goods feloniously
        stolen from one Jacob Amos Smart, Lime burner,
a silver watch, one gold seal and other articles,
he's sentenced to 14 years transportation.
Hannah's sent to the Penitentiary
        guilty of larceny only, and leaves the frame.

(*Do not forsake me, oh, my darlin' ...*)

Ice forms on bare trees and evergreens
soaring escarpments and dark, distant valleys.
        Below his window now — labourer, apothecary
at Parramatta Hospital, jack-of-all-trades —
the thin black dog of his posterity
                howls out its servitude.

The Humble Petition of Ann Rumsby

—Her Majesty's Gaol, Parramatta, 23rd August, 1822

"When William Bragge made his request
            for me, the earth didn't move one iota
        nor Heaven look on,
the appearance of Encke's Comet
over the southern hemisphere
the only propitious sign.
I found him *foul with itch; flat face, short nose*
large scars from scrofulous affection
on the right of neck and jaw
and could not like him.
All the Men servants had wished to marry me.

Sentenced to seven years transportation
on the Convict Ship *Mary Ann*
for stealing goods and chattels (value 35/-)
            from Thomas Foulsham, consigned
to the squalor of the Female Factory at Parramatta,
more miserable than any prison,
then to Dr Douglass' reformist house
        awaiting service with Judge Barron Field,
I feared that in wishing me to marry Bragge
my Master would be the ruin of me.

Halfway to the Turnpike down the Sydney Road
vexed and in tears, I met with Reverend Marsden
        (him they call 'the flogging parson')
professing himself to be my friend.
But he took up my words
in a different light to what I meant
arraigning Dr Douglass for molestation,

the social life of the Colony now afire
        with gossip and new-forged scandal.

Summonsed to court,
gaoled for perjury, refusing
to falsely incriminate my Master, banished
to Port Macquarie *because I spoke not that truth*
            as they would have it spoken,
I humbly set forth my petition."

                    *

Governor Brisbane granted Rumsby,
a female unprotected prisoner,
free pardon and sacked the magistrates.
Why she then married Bragge
remains a mystery. She vanishes into the obscurity
of private life, graves lying side by side
        in St Ann's Churchyard, Ryde, along with
Miriam, one of their eight children, roots growing
out of the scrapped cities, the adaptable sandstone,
                    generating
small rebellions here and there.

*It was, in fact, Dr Hall whom Ann met on the way to the Turnpike on that
occasion, and he passed her words on to the Rev. Marsden. To simplify the
plot details, I have taken poetic licence and conflated the two incidents.

The Marriage (1823-1850)

Set a thief to catch a thief
a rogue to catch a rogue.
I, William, became a policeman
District Constable for Melville
and then at Ryde, making prosecution
    on one occasion, of *a native of China*
being illegally on the premises of Mr Devlin,
and of various Kissing Point locals *illegally*
    selling spirits on a Sunday.

A staunch family man, not tempted
    away to the diggings by the Gold,
a marriage lasting twenty-seven years
(who ever would have thought it),
Ann ill the last six of them, *having water on the chest.*

To bed at ten o'clock, we conversed on family matters
and the sacred scriptures — she was the more devout.
    I woke at six, and saw her out of bed, by the window,
our grandchild in her arms; she came into bed again.
I said, *it rains.* She replied, *Yes it has thundered and lightened*
very much. I said, *I will set the tub to catch the water.*
In the act of putting on my socks
I heard a noise of hoarseness in her throat,
    lit the candle, and saw that she was dead.
As dispenser in the Parramatta hospital, I'd seen such deaths
— all the life drained away — and put directions in her pocket
when she had gone to Sydney with the children
    lest she should die and not be known.

The inquest over, at Mr Dowdell's Steam Boat Inn
    I trudge back home to shadows, my several lives,
to black crows fossicking in the garden
beaks plucking at their own shining feathers
or unearthing worms
        reminders of the underlying dark.
I draw the curtain-edges.

Jullian Brothers, Tightrope Walkers. 1873.

At fourteen years of age he ran away
Arthur, the second son, travelling to Sydney
            to join the circus. Years later
the tug of funambulism brought his brothers
Frederick Augustus, Edwin and Francis
        to meet him on the highwire.

High fliers, tightrope dancers,
the dream of treading air held them
            like cumulus cloud
cushioned the moment of drop,
their sling of safety hard beneath the feet
        familiar as avenues.

Their mother, Jane Ward Bragge
(rumoured to be Thunderbolt's sister)
ambushed them on the steps of Sydney Wharf
took to them with her umbrella, told them they'd disgraced
            the family name, and never to use it again.
They didn't.

Bread and Circuses

ODDFELLOWS HALL.

TO-NIGHT! TO-NIGHT!!
SATURDAY, FEB. 21.

EXHIBITION OF THE
JULLIAN
Star Variety Troupe!

Together with Signor Ferrari's
PERFORMING MONKEYS!
MONKEYS!!

The Greatest and most Versatile
Company ever in New Zealand.

LOOK OUT FOR MR EDWARD JULLIAN'S
GREAT CEILING WALKING FEAT!

– Wanganui Herald, 21 February 1874.

Travelling incognito, two tours established them
as masters of the air, gymnasts extraordinaire
        Edwin (performing as Edward), birdlike
on the flying trapeze, caught by the sure hands
        of Arthur, or doing the ceiling walk
feet hooked into loops of rope, buoyed up
by something beyond ordinary life.
Frederick Augustus billed himself as Henry.
        Arthur was always Arthur, the one who

grounded them, chased outstanding debts,
fists at the ready to give stalkers *a hammering*.

After the circus days, Arthur and Gus
started the Jullian wool-wash in Windsor,
raised families. Edwin, indecisive,
         changed his surname back and forth.
Shape-shifters, name-changers, how did they
                    come down to earth again?

George Henry Bragge (1861-1935)

He didn't join his brothers on the tightrope
        but found his own aerial flight-path
playing footy for Carlton instead,
Aussie Rules, the hurl and glide of it
not far removed from the mayhem
                      of Gaelic football.
They nicknamed him O'Shea.
In the club photo, broad-shouldered,
he's sporting the uniform
of long leather trousers and thong-laced vest,
a latter-day Oisin, mythologised.

Retired from the fray, he took up work
on the turnstiles at Carlton footy ground
drank at the pub in Racecourse Road
        with his cronies, berated by his wife
sharp-tongued Amelia (known as Lillian),
for leaving the grandsons waiting on the road
        outside, as day waned into nightfall,
not least of the traditions he established
                for future generations.

Lillian LePine (aka Amelia Matilda Austin, 1866–1937)

Not the stage-entertainer we were promised
               not even French, how dull
(we thought we were one eighth French).
Following the Norman Conquest, ambassadors
LePine/ LaPine/ LaPyne might have heralded
               something more *Moulin Rouge*.

Born in Adelaide, Amelia Matilda Austin
     married George Henry Bragge in 1885,
cleaned rental houses at South Yarra
to help the family income, looked after umbrellas
at the Caulfield Racecourse, but never gambled.
Outliving her wayward husband
by a respectable two years, buried
               in the same grave, she's registered
on her daughter's death certificate
as *Lillian* Austin. By whom?
Exit Stage Left, our star of vaudeville .

Never mind. The names Lillian and LePine
now carry on throughout the family,
               just a little bit exotic.

Augusta Jane LePine Bragge (1887-1951)

Still the puzzle remains. Who *was*
Lillian LePine, a Broadway actress perhaps?
star of music-halls or cabaret? I catch glimpses
of her peeking from the curtains
or twirling a parasol, and wonder
where the story began.

According to your daughter
and several of the sons, you yourself
sang in Adelaide's theatres, before marriage.
And here you are, immortalised
in an old family photograph, waltzing in
from the wings, corseted in breath-taking
Edwardian finery, a wedding-cake hat,
posing beside an antique vase.
Have I caught you unawares?
Lillian LePine, such a great stage name.

DNA

What's in a name? Heritage is such
a shifting concept, rooted in different soils
and cities, inimitable balance of hybrid genes
      growing and spreading like weeds.
One of my cousins wasn't stuck on family,
said, "thank god we can choose our friends."

But, needing to know
before the rising darkness, where I came from,
I spat into a test-tube and sent the sample off
      to some distant laboratory for analysis,
like trusting your heart to be weighed
at the judgement day (and not found wanting).
The answer came back: only 56% British (good),
plenty of Scandinavian input, French, German
      a smattering of Italian, Greek and Irish
and best of all, answer to a poet's prayer,
6% Iberian Peninsula, patterned in the DNA
      of distant cousins. Did Spanish smugglers
invade British shores, or sneak into the homes
of wives and daughters (descendants or forebears
of the convict Bragges)?

Like Tennyson's lotus-eaters, or Arnold's
grave Tyrian trader, who sailed to where
shy traffickers, the dark Iberians come,
      and on the beach undid his corded bales
each generation has its scholar-gypsies
its changeling children.

III

Time and Motion

I think about all the clocks, watches and sundials
I've known, their fidget-wheels and shadows,
    the clock-tower in Brisighella
its Roman numerals, abandoned T-shirt at its base
like a found poem.
My water-resistant watch that can't
    be opened to change the batteries,
the long-lost friend who made his own sundials.
Today I'm dividing past from present
like the bronze gnomon, crane-lifted
to the South Tower wall near Basser steps,
        time's shadow on the dial face.

Moon shining low through the bathroom window
the dust-corroded screen, in silvered slabs,
    gutters drumming with rain.
Sometimes in sleep I go back
to the feral, freezing high country
    the colour of first light
 to the old homes, the early locks
that held our trust.
Like refugees, we carry with us
all the forsaken places, houses
        that stood behind houses
rooms beyond rooms.

Valley of the Cycads

There are the boys, in their shiny
yellow raincoats, trekking across sand
        and riverbeds, dwarfed by
the rocky slopes, the centuries-old
                cycads, naked seeding,
growing side by side with palm trees
of the MacDonnell Ranges.

Hooded against the sky, they won't
remember much of their own journey,
        maybe the long bus-trip, but my camera
records it all, the sandstone rocks
            with water seeping through
an underground source of survival.
Wind moans through the trees

muffled thunder threatens
            another breakup of Gondwanaland,
its Mesozoic forests. What could they tell us
        these gymnosperm offspring
about the passing years, the slow slumber
watching generations creep by?
Like the giant cycads, we live and breathe

procreate, may last a hundred years.
I open the old album, made obsolete by
            electronic photographs, and the boys
are young again. Still photos
lift from the page, remembered faces
                a mixture of sunlight and dust.
How dark the shadows.

Kata Tjuta
(the Olgas)

Rising from desert sand and spinifex,
smooth red surfaces melding
into one another, like palaeocene herds,
                Kata Tjuta means 'many heads'.
Pitjantjatjara followed paths through
the massive tors, singing traditional songs
             telling stories of the Dreamtime,
caves in the lower domes once home
to the Pungalunga Men .

When Explorer Ernest Giles first saw from afar
      those *masses of rounded stones...marvellous*
in the extreme, and almost baffling description
his patron, Baron von Mueller, named them
            for Queen Olga of Würtemberg,
as though the act of naming could somehow
                 pin them down.

Standing in the Valley of the Winds
       just before sunset, we gaze and gaze
humbled by soaring monoliths that glow,
     change colour with a chameleon landscape.
Overwhelmed, the younger boy
lies face down on the boardwalk
              staring through cracks,
watches in wonder the forward march
of a trail of desert ants.

Across the river

Wrought iron trusses stretched
between Hunters Hill and Linley Point,
          the bridge took an hour to open,
four men to work the gearwheel system.
Time slowed, was somewhere else
in the tree-shaded riverscape.
You could fish there, know the tides.

Fig Tree Farm, granted to Mary Reiby
          purchased by Didier Joubert
becomes the site of Fig Tree Tea House
under the replacement bridge,
the old wheel operating the opening span
     stands memorial on the western bank
below the tangle of traffic.

Driving home, across steel and concrete
on lazy summer afternoons
          you catch glimpses of the river.

East Coast by Night

Always driving, in the dark between two places
           as though this is a dream
the same journey, which you will wake up from
           back at the sign of Pegasus
and all your life before you
           drawn on by a clipped-back moon.

Clouds stack and shift on the horizon
           past childhood's forgotten townships
the years between an interval of sleep
           the darkness you travel in
to each successive coastline
           cold dawn in which you arrive.

Beyond each loss
           you stand upon the cliff again
           facing a vaster ocean, unshrinkable
caught between thoughts, between stars
           outside time, a nameless opiate
as though you might have died
           and yet you wake.

Keeping your head above water

The water, once you're into it, is all there is.
Tides from Antarctica come in clear and clean,

freezing until you surrender. The waves
are huge, currents crossing each other

like ascending mountains, you need to push
up and up, float free, carried like flotsam.

If you think of it as water, you may drown.
It is, simply, another medium,

horizontal slash of waves meeting shore.
Snapshots of life flash by, like a PowerPoint

display. Sometimes, negotiating breakers,
you catch glimpses of the lost world

knowing it for a chimera. Out there it's euphoria
the rock and massage of the wild seas, you are

and are not there, in a selkie's skin, called back
eventually to the everyday, that other

life, beyond surf pounding on the breakwater,
the moment of high tide.

Bicycle path in rain

This morning the black cockatoos
looked like sodden rags, hanging
    motionless on storm-wire fences.

By the time you've completed a circuit
they're gone, leaving only their shadow
    the echo of flight.

Rain lies like a groundsheet reflection
the length of the netball court, puddles
    are stacked saucers of light.

Dog-walkers wearing anoraks carry leashes
and umbrellas, take shelter, only wet dogs
    and mad cyclists out in this weather.

Under cover, the small Chinese group
practising t'ai chi to tape-recorded music
    recall the lingering sound

of reed-pipe players in a Beijing park
the slow, graceful movements of martial art.
    At the top of the hill you pause

in the cloak of wind, to remove fogged glasses
wipe the mirror, strip off damp gloves
    feeling skeletal bone beneath the skin

a fragility you can't encapsulate in words,
untamed as peeling bark or winter trees
    shedding their burden of leaves.

Valediction

(for Martin Harrison)

Born in Stars, We Live on Earth as Poets
– William Blake

Amidst petitions for Sunday's rally against climate change
    education cuts, and all the other head-in-sand
        disasters promoted by a Machiavellian
government, an email arrives, telling me you've died.
        All your life on hold, a memory
before you become the vessel of your words.
"Poetry is the key to experience," you said.

Choosing "Seeing Paddocks" for the anthology
        from poems you'd sent, discovering you
through your created landscape, I found a heart attuned
    to *the earth dream, the land dream,* and was glad.
Some things disturb perception, flicker of shadow
        and untruth, like emptiness, a car's slipstream
the placement of death.

Driving past the out-of-kilter façade of UTS
        on Broadway, I will always think of you
one day reading in Gould's Book Arcade
    or talking to students, the next, found by the roadside
near Brooklyn, your generous heart stilled, Wollombi home
        quiet, awaiting your return.

        Before our dust
goes back to glittering stars, we will journey again
        through the no-longer-green forests
and grieve with you, numb elegiacs watering
        a dry landscape. In a broken planet
we have to say what's true.

Vale, John Upton (1939-2017)

I'm reading through your final manuscript
the witty poems, clever images, well-wrought
phrases, seldom personal except in sudden
        uncaught moments. Some poems
are out of place or needing more attention —
you won't like to hear this, I know, but
the craftsman in you will listen.
Ten minutes later the phone-call comes
                telling me you've died.

You knew the end was near, but never when,
rarely talked about it, only confronting
the process through poetry, wry, hard-hitting
metaphors like tempered steel, rays and needles,
the death-defying kiss of a machine
        all subject-matter for a dauntless muse.

You were independent, self-contained,
a penchant for chocolates softening your austerity.
I will miss our email repartee, your fierce critical
presence at poetry meetings, even the shouts of
"the language is *ordinary*!" I will remember you
arriving in baseball cap, or panama
        up until the last, writing for dear life.

The final poem in your manuscript
I thought was wrongly placed, a dream in which
your wife came back to wake you, for a cup of tea.
You told her she was dead. She argued, poured the tea,
you brought her up to speed. It seemed an afterthought
                but now I know you knew.

Gurrumul (1971-2017)

Singing of *Bayini*, strangers who came
    for the trepang, first visitors to our shores,
families sit together on the beach, gather
    like clouds, in the shadow of paperbarks.

White cockatoos fly over the clay pans
flapping their wings, the rustling of ducks
as they preen feathers, rippling the water
    among lily pads, smell of the mud,
mud bubbling with the drift of water,
      catfish, tortoises.

To have travelled the world and returned
untouched by acclaim, the crowds and freeways,
borne only by the music. The booming swell
    of waves, the bay now awash with foam,
sounds of spray hissing back from the crest.
Hanging in hammocks on the verandah,
alert to the storm-front. Not fearing a dark
    you cannot see. Feeling the shadow.

The rocking of waves that enters sleep, as
you swim down from wakefulness, a skein
    of mist across the cliffs.

Never to have seen your island, but know it
by the feel of sand, rough grains that sift
    through fingers, trickling like time,
prescience of the orange-footed scrub fowl
pecking away at seed, the wind among grasses.

To sing of it.

Winter Pear Tree

Snow lies like a question
across the Bibbenluke landscape
      ponderous and eternal
as though Spring might not come.

White hills, bare branches, shed
so much light, the conifers watchful
guarding low, snow-topped walls
      birds gone from the garden.

Only the firs bear foliage
the pear tree bowed beneath its icy burden
    in silent wonder, its old mystique
the centre of everything.

The Prodigal

I watch winter taking the city,
the way it scavenges the husks of light,
                    throws down shadows
in doorways, stairwells, under bridges,
          and I grieve for what has been lost.

In the bare hospital room
          nuns came by sometimes
officious blackbirds, pecking
at the rumpled sheets
                silencing my screams.
You were the first-born, first swimmer
in those turbulent seas.

As a toddler no fence could contain you,
          you'd climb over barbed wire
to get to the road; later, there were lost
T-shirts and thrown-away lunches,
                trips to Emergency.
Through it all I loved you, the difficult
HSC years, pregnancy tests, magic mushrooms,
travel from Bangkok to Nepal
                    to find yourself.

There was always a path through the mountain
a campervan waiting in the forest
                    for your return.

At first my lifestyle didn't matter,
          you and the new boyfriend approved us
drank our whisky, loved the children
until he found God, and took you with him.

You came to my house with books
                    and pamphlets, information
on conversion therapy, urging me to repent.
You ask me to think of these things
on my *downward path to the grave.*
But for me there's no better place
                    than this, here, now.

Kirribilli by night

The house is quiet now
children asleep, even the one
            who keeps her night-light on,
fearing the populous dark.
A planet's dust, metallic,
                alive, is sifted down.

You tiptoe downstairs
in blindfold darkness, brush against
            whitewashed walls, avoiding
the minefield of bags and boxes
filled with their daily lives. Ceiling fans
    creak listlessly, disperse the day's heat.

Down by the harbour
the Opera House broods in cathedral shadow,
        bats querulous in the Moreton Bays.
Lovers walk hand in hand, past winding streets
the high, narrow houses, not knowing
                the moment of their parting.

Alone now, on the edge of sleep
you drowse towards morning, dreaming
            of past houses, always in disarray,
of other children. A foghorn sounds
from the 5 a.m ferry, light creeps
                through the white shutters.

Lavender Bay in rain

(to watch or see is secret,
to spy, to peep, to pry into
the rain…)

Once Quiberee — Aboriginal for fresh spring of water
— then called Hulk Bay, sometimes Phoenix Bay
after the prison ship moored there,
                    it now takes its name
from the boatswain, George Lavender.

From his window Brett saw
the sodden palm trees drooping in slow rain
                    framed by the open pane
like white ships' masts
as he painted the browned-out edges
        of its little leisure-craft.

For years the foreshore view was overgrown
a dead-end dump for rubbish,
                for superseded trains and derelicts.
Wendy's secret garden recreates
        a forgotten past: natives, exotics, towering
fig-trees, run along winding gully paths
in the shadow of office towers,
where owls, parrots, wagtails mingle cries.

Walking with friends in the garden
(the small black dog securely on his leash)
            easy to imagine the wildness
that once was the life of this bay
                through sixty thousand years,
to pry beyond the rain.

Brief* Garden

*Here I sit, in my lamplit bungalow, with the warm thick rain drumming
on the roof and leaking through the holes, with a glass of gin...
and from the boys' quarters the tentative tooting of flutes.'*

(Donald Friend, *Diaries*, 13th May 1958)

We turn off from the Galle Road
to the Bawa Estate and its tropical house
enshrined as a gallery. Here a riot
    of rainforest gardens, random fountains,
the famed satyr gateposts, usher you in.

Friend's mural's a paean to one-time Ceylon,
a jubilant mapping of palace and temples, of village
    and street scenes, rickshaws and umbrellas,
monks with their begging-bowls.
Spotted deer roam freely, elephants, tusked
    and bejewelled, jostle for pride of place.
Nude Krishna pipes music from a reed flute
as we stray into his paradise.

Then to the courtyard and clay wall tiles
    incised with elephants and strutting peacocks
ancient hunters, chariots, and swan-necked ships.
Sculptures survive, and rough engravings
    on concrete garden seats, of monkeys,
a boy sleeping, unmindful of watchers
one of the many boys.

After dark, it's 'Brief' at its best. Monsoon rains over,
an enormous full moon floods the garden with light
the night full of fireflies. But the climate's now taking
      its toll of the mural wall, floors cracked
and subsiding, the colours sinking from sight.

* The property, bequeathed to Bevis Bawa by his mother, was gained
through a successful legal brief.

IV

The Pearl Divers

They remind you of astronauts
lumbering into another dimension
      in those cumbrous suits, heavy
as the weight of a man, brass helmets
museum pieces now.

Stepping through the wide rubber collar,
      two sailors as tenders to help him,
he pushes his feet along wrinkling canvas
dons the copper breastplate, sharp edges
 digging into shoulders and neck.

Wrestling the collar into place,
      they anchor the clamps, tighten
with T wrenches. Then the belt, lead-weighted,
leather straps crossed at the chest
base of helmet screwed into breastplate,
      visor closed and sealed, like armour.

He enters the water backwards
from the ship's ladder, finding each rung
      with the metal tip of a shoe,
holds the descending line
as the harbour swallows him.

Weightless now, he feels himself sliding
      towards nothingness, floating
in a void, the dark of nightmares.
Imagines himself cut off, alone,
the nitrogen bubbles trapped in his blood
pushing through soft tissues. Men bleed
      from eyes, nose, ears. Or the squeeze,

the diver squashed by the ocean's pressure
                              into the helmet he wore.

Native bare-pelt divers mill round him
many of them women, some pregnant.
Descending on the one breath, they prise
      shells from the rock ledges, stowing them
in string bags, rise slowly to the surface
                          dribbling air from their lungs.
Then he's walking on the bottom
                    of the sea, euphoric, flying,
breathing underwater, oyster beds choked
with the gigantic shells.

The Moon via telescope

1. Annular eclipse of the sun. 29th April, 2014

A thoroughly bizarre eclipse, mostly visible
            to penguins in Antarctica
the blood-red sun sinking between trees
the moon a black disk biting in
        part of its shadow
                just missing Earth.

2. Occultation of Saturn. 14th May, 2014

It's at its brightest, all oval-shaped storms
        and frozen rings, particles of rock and ice
whirling forever like a fairground Ferris wheel.
From your back verandah
focussed on Saturn racing away from the moon
    the bent moon rising and rising
                criss-crossed with black branches
            its craters visible from here, we feel it.
The absence of stars, shifting emptiness of space
harks back to the big nothing.

3. In all its phases.

Since Apollo 11 and Armstrong's moon-walk
(and was it a fake after all?)
the moon boasts no old man, or even giant rabbits
but has its craters, valleys, mountains, seas
its *Mare Cognitum* and *Serenitatis.*
I saw icy wind-carved peaks

and down through hidden valleys
tumbled shelves of rock, fringed with hanging icicles
    like long white teeth, ravines so deep and black
a wind-eaten bridge of stone, nothing
but space on either side, the mountains
      folding back upon themselves.

Skywatchers

As we climb the dim-lit verges
of Observatory Hill, once Windmill Hill
bicycle lamps whirl past like fireflies,
         orbiting in the dark
 city kids kick-boxing or exercising
   in green space, lights blinking on the Bridge.
We set up telescopes.

The sky is picketed with stars
a gibbous moon, its bent man bundling sticks,
      a far-off plane, moving slowly, glowing
like a rogue planet. The lit-up time ball
that drops each afternoon at 1 pm
                  towers behind us
no longer calibrating ships' chronometers
but accurate to the second.

The Emu in the Sky's defined by nebulae
           hundreds of light years away
visible against our Milky Way, body and legs
the trailing dust lanes to Scorpius, head resting
in the Coalsack dark nebula, a map to the Universe.
Once seen, like a Rorschach ink-blot
     the night sky will never look the same again.

Far below, Fiona Hall's
    Folly for Mrs Macquarie, a filigree of cages
in Sydney Sculpture Walk, Botanic Gardens
images a self-imposed confinement
       barbed wire, an axe, some bones
a domed roof of Norfolk Island pine
too brittle to make excellent ships masts.

The Travelling Telescopes

The great river flows
From the mountains to the sea
I am the river, the river is me.
                    – Maori proverb.

Polynesians came from the sea
a thousand years ago
                    in long canoes, ferrying
as well as crops and grain, their telescopes
for hunting and navigation,
                    the Wanganui River catchment
a sacred settlement for Maori.

In England 1857, Isaac Fletcher commissioned
Thomas Cooke to build a refractor telescope,
                    set up Tarn Bank Observatory
to research double stars.
The peripatetic telescope changed hands
when Fletcher died, was moved to Worsley
         then down-under, shipped to Joseph Ward
in Wanganui, across the Tasman Sea.

Massive stars live fast, die young
sometimes become black holes or dwarf stars
         survived by fainter, invisible companions
sometimes gas from the dying star
                    glows with ultra-violet radiation.
Maori legends tell another story
         of Sirius (*Takurua*) and his pale sky-brother

once carried by god *Kewa* in a basket of stars
    for planting in *Te Ikaroa*, the Milky Way
their rise now marking the changing of seasons
        chill onset of winter.

Other Worlds

A neanderthal handprint, eons old
        marks the cave wall
an understanding of time,
        some idea of the seasons, a future
to make the darkness visible
like Bede's lone sparrow, flying

        securely from the lit-up meadhall
           into this unknown silence;
the parallel sighting of a bird of paradise
its ruddy plumes aflame
        destined to vanish into the mass of green.
Inbuilt, this need for some afterword:

De Quiros in another century
        voyaging towards the South Land
          his vision and obsession;
William Lane's utopian dream
        a new-world colony in Paraguay
Nueva Australia, then Cosme, further south.

Mormon settlers crossed the Mojave desert
        in search of salvation and a promised land.
The seed vault of icy Longyearbyen
        was built to preserve a food-store's DNA
          for 20,000 years
if galaxies or climates don't collide.

New worlds swim into our sight
        like hedgerow prominences on the sun,
we need the 'glint' or rainbows from their oceans
        the sign of water in their atmosphere.

Kepler 438b is one of these, 475 light years away
        perhaps our 'twin', a double indemnity?

I dream a transit life, the air (blue, or a shade thereof)
is filled with plastic drones (like particle bubbles)
    collecting information. Thinking to move to where
the grass (if it exists) is greener, to a galactic
            urban sprawl beyond the crowded CBD?
                    Get in before the rush.

Earth Hour

Night
and the lights go out in the world
        (or some of them do).
Empty offices still burn the midnight oil
and the neighbours, climate sceptics
        are staging their own light-show.

We douse the basecamp lantern, settle down
to watch the gyroscope of stars
        whirling unbroken like a desert sky,
alert to night-noises, whirr of insects
        the fragrance of frangipani
lingering in a garden.

New galaxies appear before our gaze
millions of light years away
        unknown planets, the ultracool dwarfs
to be marvelled at, perhaps, by future eyes.
        Space monkeys, doomed to orbit
Mars forever, might disagree.

Warning lamps on the Bridge blink off and on
off and on, familiar as the Harbour's rhythms
        importunate as a draft-card.
Unblinking, the city switches itself back on
        for yet another year, or ninety-nine,
in harness to the sold-off 'poles and wires'.

V

Drought

It begins as it will end
reliving the scene you created
   without grass, stone, leaves.

The sky's a shepherd's warning
reddened with dust, framework
of a corrugated-iron shack
standing like a giant harp
        wired to the wind, in this
inhospitable country, the roof
a pleated tin accordion, playing out
some half-remembered tune
from a 'forties back-bar, as the iron
        enters your soul.

Trees warp with pain, simulating
the death-throes of dinosaurs
lumbering out of the first ice-age
into this unholy desert
      hardening to fossils

spectres of a superseded landscape.

Mungo Man

(unearthed 1974, returned to tribal elders 17 Nov. 2017)

Lake Mungo, dried-out since the last Ice Age
might remind you of
        craters of the moon, its serrated dunes
like ghostly turrets, towering above
a furrowed and sand-raked valley.
Bones of the tall man lay
red ochre covered,
            legs outstretched, hands crossed,
as though in ritual burial.

Undisturbed for 50,000 years
                in that long dreaming
when rainfall seeped
across the Dividing Range,
fish abundant in the waters
        a landscape where megafauna
roamed for the taking.

Returned now to the place of exhumation
        repatriated, his bones receive
no promised sanctuary. Each gust of wind,
        each erosion, strips another layer
from the gouged and arid earth.

West Antarctic Ice Sheet

Ice that trapped Shackleton and crushed his ship
ice the crew camped on until the spring
                    hoping to drift to Paulet Island,
the floes that proved impassable
all are melting now, faster and faster
                    locked into a process already begun.
Shackleton gave Frank Hurley his mittens
suffering frostbite himself, so the photographer
             could walk into his frozen image
as though part of some vanishing point
in another century —
like the merging of parallel lines.

Beyond the history of their names
             we step out into drifts of hail
the size of boulders, floods
and gale-force winds, billions of tons of ice
flowing faster than snowfall replenishes.
The Bay of Whales ceases to exist
when an iceberg breaks off from Ross ice shelf.
             An extra five metres added to sea levels
will make of our coastline another Atlantis
submerged buildings and motorways,
             a memory of the lost ship *Endurance*
disappearing beneath the waves.

The Larsen Ice Shelf

"Each day Humble* supplies enough energy to melt
7 million tons of glacier." (Feb. 2, 1962)

Warned of the giant rift
　　　　　threatening to split the ice shelf,
the collapse of polar sea-ice, rising
sea levels, the company's not-so-humble
boast comes true, an iceberg twice
the size of Samoa now calved
　　　　　into the South Atlantic Ocean.

In the weird southern light, in blistering
cold, dry ice on the decks of passing ships,
　　crags to each side of them, Carl Larsen,
master of the Norwegian whaler *Jason*,
sailed past that sculpted ice front
from Cape Longing to Heard Island,
　　　　　stunned by its fringing bays.

As the sea rises in a green wall
striped with foam, flecked with snow,
　　　　　burning fossil fuels
have melted the first two sections, the third
and most massive broken away,
its changing contours
　　　　　shattered like safety glass.

* A company division of Exxon.

Hubbard Glacier

The land's barricade thickens,
        advances towards the gulf
in a frozen season

ice blue as blown glass
or ammonite shell
        calves off like bubble-foam

you hear it split
broken floes drift by the boat,
a migration of fish, birds, mammals
            the drag hook of memory

the green part of you that
        never leaves, gathers it all in,
a chimera of light.

Somewhere, sea-lions stretch out
on a rocky island, as the world
        that survives grows smaller.

Broken Ocean

*"What was missing was the cries of seabirds that surrounded
the boat on previous voyages...."*
— Ivan Macfadyen, yachtsman.

In the past we'd seen birds   following the boat
resting on our mast like sentinels
                or wheeling in the distance
                                feeding on pilchards.
The birds were missing because there were no fish
no sound but wind in the rigging   waves knocking
against the hull the steady thud of debris.

Now a mother-ship's trawling the reef
stripping it   day after day
                working at night under floodlight.
We feared pirates   but Melanesian men
came alongside with gifts   sugar-bags full of fish.
All they wanted was tuna   the rest dumped as rubbish
                in the maw of that rotting sea.

After we left Japan   lights of small moored ships at its edges
battered freighters and patrol boats   the ocean itself was dead
                the shape of a tumorous whale rolled on the surface
like the dome of an old Buddhist stupa
or an alien power-plant.

Power-poles snapped off by the last killer wave   trail wires
in the middle of the ocean   yellow plastic buoys   synthetic rope
fishing lines and nets   our propeller entangled
                as though in a mangrove swamp.
No turtles dolphins flurries of birds
or sharks   for 3,000 nautical miles.

In the waters above Hawaii   you could see right into the depths
            skeletal as xray artworks   collages of modernity
debris all the way down   soft-drink bottles
pieces of junk the size of a truck   a factory chimney
sticking out of the water.
            Sailing through this garbage dump   plastic and flotsam
scraping the length of the boat

we'd push for a fleet to clean up the mess
if environmental damage   from burning the fuel
            wasn't worse than just leaving it there.

Vanua Levu Island, Fiji

He paces a few steps, crouches before
    a silvery tideline, hands beginning
to dig the black sand. *This is the post*
of my old house, he says. In the 1960s
it stood back from the seaside
where he'd jump the narrow estuary
and run past mangrove forests,
          fringed coconut palms, to school.

With summer's king tides advancing,
a broad tongue of shallow water
          spilling across the land
the children had to swim to school,
families without boats built rafts
the poor man's ark —
to leave their houses, foundations warping
        in the salty soil.

The village was on the move.
At the new site, thirty green bungalows
    dot the hillside, gardens and fish farms
keep them busy, more villages earmarked
to relocate, like the old woman
who carries the sun
        and the moon in her string bag
to plant in the sky.

Below, abandoned structures remain
      as the jungle slowly swallows them;
a warped door flaps open, the canted ribcage
of the old school eaten away by salt
and tropical damp. Trees are few, branches
strewn like giant bird bones, rising sea levels
        erode the tangled roots.
How high the mountain.

The Doomsday Vault

Svalbard, planet earth's most northern community
has long polar nights, their only light the full moon
and reflective snow, the dark months
    a twilight zone, sun always hidden
below the dead horizon
  of glaciers and snowfields, the only vegetation
sparse dwarf birch and tiny polar willow.

No roads connect the settlements, snowmobiles
do the job, or aircraft, sometimes boats
    if pack ice doesn't stop them.
Svalbard houses the global seed belt
drilled into the top of the world, genetic codes
    contained in boxes of frozen soil
for crop diversity, 800,000 different seeds.

Now it's the summer solstice, 99 days
    of the midnight sun that never sets
moving through 360 degrees, spiralling
    higher and higher, its overheated images
photographic reflections, caught in the grid of water
energy riding on buoyant plumes of gas
    and the permafrost is thawing.

The Domesday Book, William the Conqueror's
   survey of England, meant the beginning
of village history, a reckoning, their fiefs described −
dimensions, ploughing capacity, number of agricultural
workers, their mills, fishponds, value in pounds.
Not doom, the facing up to the record
    from which there's no appeal.

In an unpredictable climate
   the terms mean much the same.

Forty-one degrees

Almost summer, season of hot dry winds.
Cooling off in Clovelly Bay, among
sea-urchins and blue gropers, you enter
          a floating world, easy to forget
out there it's another heatwave.
Outside my townhouse, men with hats
and overheated brains are repairing
     the roof, damaged in last April's storms,
still leaking water.

The garden needs watering. While rock-plants
and veldt daisies may survive
               into our future desert, magnolias
bloom fast and quickly die, browned flowers
          drifting onto unswept tiles. At dusk
the air's still warm, black cockatoos have fled
with raucous cry, back to their cooler forests.
In a neighbouring pond, frogs belt out
     loud mating-songs, secure for now, until
developers arrive, to move the earth.

Out there, it's also a war on terror
as jihadists and extremists take control
and suddenly we know
          how, at any given moment,
in a train carriage in London, a music festival
in Paris, or a Lindt cafe somewhere
     life can be snatched away.
Même pas mal, say the French, in solidarity,
"Not even hurt." But we all are.

In this hot, shifting darkness
       I wish the rains would come.

The Phantom Trees

"We're building tomorrow's Sydney. Conveniently located stops."
— Government signage
"You may be assured planning approval for this project includes strategies to minimise its impact on existing vegetation and the environment."
—Minister for Transport and Infrastructure

It never ends, this extinction of the planet, until it ends.
Yes, there is outrage. We wrote letters, signed petitions
attended rallies and demos, reinvented ourselves on xerox.
On Valentine's Day we sent a floral heart
to that tin man, our Premier
                 but the answer came back the same:
two trees to be planted for every small tree removed,
eight for every "significant" tree, to arrive on trucks
bulk delivered, for mass plantings, silhouetting
                      a pre-determined landscape.

Will they be Moreton Bays, eucalypts, Port Jackson Figs
        or designer trees, fast-growing patio plants
(preferably not native) to break up the ugliness
of railway tracks and concrete high-rise? Few of us
will be here to see the outcome, stand in vanishing shade,
breathe thinner oxygen, in a photosynthesis
                  more intricate than lungs.

Phantom trees like shadowy stage-props
burgeoning at the edges of their minds.

Bonsai and Penjing Collection
(National Arboretum, Canberra)

Beyond the lakeside café, you enter a world
of miniature trees and forests —
art imitating life, mimicking the size
      of full-grown trees — or is it life
sculpted, transformed to artefact?

Some trees grow slant, windswept
buffeted into obedience. Others,
      informal upright, show visible curves
in trunk and branches, like contorted limbs.
Trees cascade over water or down
        mountain sides, roots flourishing
in soil between the rocks, as in
Japanese landscapes. You imagine clouds
        and misty peaks, figurines
(monks, animals) dotting the lower slopes.

Like a bizarre Photoshop
the tiny Banksia bears her burden
of full-sized, heavy-lidded banksia men
        forever lurking in shadows.
Shari portray trees in their struggle to live,
trunks bare of bark, the way we work
and rework the past, defoliating memory,
        clamping and wiring.

Gnarled roots of the eucalypt
form Tolkien faces, twisted with pain,
        spirit-houses for the dead
or prison-trees.

Powerful Owl (*Ninox strenua*)

Hunched on the backyard fence
    at dusk, gatekeeper of the night
silhouetted against the sky
        you watch us, sonic hearing

an inner light. You belong
    in bushland, or forest reserves
feathers carved out of mud flats
        and river tides, grey-brown
above dark v-shaped chevrons
wings drilled for flight, sharp talons
        triggered for prey.

Eyes are deep water holes
in your facial mask, luminous orbs
        the seers of our captivity.
Harbinger of sorrows, or avatar
once nesting in tree hollows formed
over hundreds of years, you vanish
        on currents of air.

Sea Dog

Out on the Harbour
in the wooden yacht without a sail
Heathcliff, the little black dog
          in his flotation-jacket, balances
on the prow, John-Howard eyebrows scan
the horizon like sensors, nose uplifted, snuffing
the breeze, a captain searching for landfall.
    You'd almost expect to hand him a telescope.

We anchor offshore from a sandy bay —
the water's fine, and passing monoliths
    wave a greeting, foreshores as thickly wooded
as a Glover painting, except for Darling Harbour.
Take your last look at Barangaroo, before
the casino's phallic projection, burgeoning
          in metal, marks another dispossession,
high-rollers blowing smoke-screens.

Every dog has his day, so they say.

Beyond Head of Bight

Matthew Flinders charted this coast
                stunned by its loveliness.
Unending Bunda cliffs, towering over a vast
unspoiled ocean, iconic curve the longest line
        of sea-cliffs in the world; a nursery for
sea lion colonies to raise their pups,
seasonal home of the southern right whales
    great white sharks, humpbacks, bluefish tuna
white-bellied sea eagle, and albatross.
                    What's not to save?

The ocean's a rich field for profiteers,
                for oil and gas, offshore drilling,
underwater blasts of seismic exploration.
Remember the Gulf of Mexico Oil Spill
(2010 Deepwater Horizon), oil pouring
           into the sea for eighty-seven days?

Seasonal upwelling of deep ocean waters
along the coast brings nutrients to the surface,
               fertility, making it a hotspot.
Southern right whales come here to Head of Bight
from summer feeding grounds in the Antarctic
    to calve and breed, not feeding until their return.
Spy hopping, deep diving, the calves now schooled
in life skills, from a distance they look
like upturned hulls, a constant loop of broad gun-metal
        backs, their sheen a light across oceans.

And now the Reef

Flowers turned to stone! Not all the botany
Of Joseph Banks, hung pensive in a porthole,
Could find the Latin for this loveliness...
– Slessor, "Five Visions of Captain Cook"

For them it was unassailable
                    an inferno of sea and sharp coral
a Venus fly-trap drawing them in. Fragile
was never the word for this underwater forest
            of blooms, at low tide a vertical hedge
of skeletal rock, holding *Endeavour* to ransom.

Off Heron Island, incandescent
chameleon colours once visible from space,
by night the Reef's a construction site
            for marine cities, a limestone world,
the coral polyps always building, never leaving
            the safety of their homes except to feed.

The reefs outside support both predator
      and prey, in an intricate dance of survival.
                  Cleaner-fish congregate at thriving
cleaning-stations, like a suburban car-wash,
to eat dead skin and parasites
      from manta rays already queued for service.

Seahorses change colour and texture, matching
            the coral they cling to for protection.
Once a year, at full moon, great ribbons
            of coral spawn drift on the tide, most
to be eaten by fish. Enough survive. Or would
if you *could* put the Barrier Reef in a glass box.

Bleaching, the crystal tines turn ghostly white
and fade, like flowers dying.

Before our Earth falls silent

While there are still trees along the avenue
                    a canopy of branches
their muted voices singing in the wires,
the giant eucalypt outside my window
        an orchestra in the wind, I will walk through
the sunlight and shadow of the tree-tops

                    the softness of earth beneath
pretending it's all unchanged.
The black cockatoos preening each others'
            beaks and feathers, like lovers, are gone
currawongs and warblers vanished.
I'd never longed for the wake-up call
                of birdsong, until it ceased.

                    I will go back down to the bay
to swim among sea urchins and schools of fish
                    to marvel at rock pools at low tide
a water-Garden of Earthly Delights
sea anemones and psychedelic nudibranch
        strange mutants from an LSD trip gone wrong
as though already touched by chemical waste.

Giant crabs climb the rock-face
                    hide their rusting prehistoric bodies
from probing fingers,
                    entanglement of seaweed.
At twilight, moths come drifting
fall out of sight behind trees.
Blue fish flicker like gas flames
                jump from your hands.

Acknowledgments

Poems in this collection have appeared in the following publications:

As Far As The Eye Can See (DiVerse, 2014), *Australian Poetry Journal* (3.1 and 4.1), *Australian Poetry Anthology* (2014, 2015, 2016 and 2018), *II.15* (Poetry Sydney, 2015), *Caring for Country* (Phoenix Education, 2017), *Hope for Whole - eBook* (*Plumwood Mountain*, vol.5, no.2, 2018), *Lane Cove Literary Awards 2016* and *2018*, *Live Encounters Poetry & Writing* (Feb., 2018), *Poetry and Place Anthology* (Close-Up Books, Melbourne, 2015), *Quadrant*, *Southerly*, *Guide to Sydney Rivers* (ed. Susan Adams and Les Wicks, 2015), *Sri Lanka Journey* (Ginninderra, 2017), *The Best Australian Poems 2017* (Black Inc.), *The Canberra Times*, *The Drawings − Drysdale* (DiVerse, 2012), *tremble* (International Poetry Studies Institute, 2016), *Wild* (Ginninderra, 2018), *www.cordite.com*, *www.plumwoodmountain.com*.

'The Black Line' won first prize in the Banjo Paterson Award for Open Poetry 2015; 'Earth Hour' won first prize in the national Earth Hour poetry competition 2014. Several other poems were shortlisted for awards.

A number of the poems in this collection found their inspiration in the work of Australian artists, as follows:

'Across the river': Herbert Reginald Gallop, *Fig Tree Bridge, Lane Cove.* 1940s.
'Drought': Russell Drysdale, *Study for Drought series, 1945.*
'Lavender Bay in rain': Brett Whiteley, *Lavender Bay in the rain, 1978.* Epigraph appears below the artist's stamp.
'Winter Pear Tree': Lucy Culliton, *Winter pear tree, 2009.*